Start-Up Terminology
A good natured guide to talking the talk

Techno-Babble

Jargon

HYPERBOLE

Legalese

Double speak

Start-Up Company Terminology

Start-up businesses have their own special vocabulary which a founder, funder, vendor, employee or director must understand and use with skill. Speaking fluent start-up is particularly important when seeking external investors or sophisticated industry partners.

Here are some of the more frequently used terms that you may encounter:

ABC   Acronym for anti bribery and corruption. Businesses dealing with government contracts, large money transfers or wagering are expected to have policies, processes and controls to detect and prevent corrupt practices.

Accelerator (aka Incubator)

A center where start-ups are "incubated" through mentorship, space and sometimes cash. A mixture of an intensive care unit and a school for founders.

Accredited Investor (aka Sophisticated investor)

A rich individual potentially interested in investing in your company. Or, more technically, according to the SEC: "A natural person with income exceeding $200,000 in each of the two most recent years or joint income with spouse exceeding $300,000 for those years and a reasonable expectation of the same income level in the current year; or A natural person who has individual net worth, or joint net worth with the person's spouse, that exceeds $1 million at the time of the purchase, excluding the value of the primary residence of such person." What this means for your start-up is you must require potential investors to prove that they can afford to risk their money in your start-up, in order to comply with the law.

Agile

Also sometimes referred to as 'Lean' or 'Lean thinking' and strongly related to 'Lean Start-up' (see below). A business methodology for getting quick progress by approaching work as a series of short (typically 90 day) projects.

AGM

Acronym for annual general meeting. Companies that have multiple shareholders are required to provide a forum in which the shareholders can receive reports on how the company is performing and what prospects it may have and at which shareholders may vote for directors or resolutions to enable the company to pursue a desired course of action. Sometimes referred to as an ordinary general meeting (OGM) or just GM.

AI Acronym for artificial intelligence. Not to be confused with the acronym for artificial insemination!

aka Acronym = Also known as

AML (aka anti-money laundering) Policies, procedures and controls implemented to prevent your platform or business model from being used to 'legitimise' proceeds of crime by 'washing' them through a genuine business. Specially important if your business moves money in large quantities, internationally, or between users whose identities are not thoroughly vetted.

Angel investors (aka Angels or Business Angels)

People who specialise in investing in early stage ventures. The often work together in groups and frequently provide contacts, mentoring and business advice to the founders and staff of the companies in which they invest. Sometimes referred to as 'micro VCs'.

ASIC

Australian Securities and Investments Commission. ASIC is an independent Commonwealth department/body which regulates Australia's corporate, markets and financial services sectors. The SEC is the USA counterpart.

Bandwidth

Originally a measure of the ability of an internet connection to pass data. Currently sometimes used as a collective noun for the resources needed to implement a strategy.

Beneficial Owner

A beneficial owner ultimately owns or controls a shareholder or customer and/or the natural person on whose behalf a transaction is being conducted.

BHAGs

Big Hairy Audacious Goals – stretch targets.

Bleeding Edge

So far ahead of the current market that the company is not expected to make a profit (hence the phrase 'bleeding cash') for many years. In this growth phase companies need to raise new capital to fund growth and development because they cannot sustain themselves with their own generated cashflows.

Boot-Strapping

Using money generated by the business itself (or sometimes by "friends and family") to get the business going.

B-to-B — Business to Business: A company that sells products and/or services to other companies.

B-to-C — Business to Consumer: A company that sells products and/or services to individual (or retail) consumers.

Burn Rate (aka Run Rate) — How fast the company is using up its cash reserves. It's not unusual for a start-up to lose large sums of money for several years before breaking even, or making a profit. Should be measured in $/year or $/month. Will indicate the amount of time available before capital raising is required.

Business plan — Describes and costs the planned activities at each point in time projected forwards from the current date.

CEO

Acronym for Chief Executive Officer. The most senior executive in the business. Usually this is the person who is running the day to day operations of the business. It is not necessary for the CEO to be a board member although they usually attend all board meetings and report to the board. Many CEOs are board members and should technically be called 'Managing Directors'.

Chairman

A board member who is generally considered to be 'the boss of the board'. This is the person who has the strongest relationship with the CEO and also the one who represents the company to the investment community. It is generally considered a good idea if the Chairman is not the same person as the CEO/MD.

Churn Rate

Customers lost usually expressed as a percentage of the total number of customers. Sometimes expressed as a percentage of new customers gained. This is a measure of 'Stickiness' or the ability of the business model to retain customers. Churn rate decreases growth. Churn rate should always be lower than acquisition rate if the company is growing. usually subsequent to acquisition in a subscription-based business model

Cliff

Usually applies steps in vesting schedules for shares given to employees over time. Cliffs are often used by investors to make sure the CEO sticks around after getting their investment; leave before the shares have vested and loose the entitlement – leave after and take a substantial equity stake.

Chair

The person who chairs the board. Ideally this should be a person whom the directors and senior executives respect and who can speak for the board with authority and knowledge.

Compliance

The discipline of making sure that a company conforms to the appropriate national and international rules of conduct, both in their internal operations and their dealings with third parties. It is not a luxury or an optional extra.

Consent to Act

A document that should be signed by a prospective director prior to being appointed. It signifies that the signatory understands and accepts the liabilities, duties and obligations of directorship.

Constitution (aka memorandum or articles of incorporation)

A document that sets out the rules governing the relationship between the company and its shareholders. Typically this will be a standard form document and will detail how directors are elected, how the AGM will be run, what matters may be decided by the board (and subsequently delegated to management if the board so wish) and what must be voted upon by the shareholders.

Controlling Ownership

The concept of control is not necessarily a 51% shareholding. Voting rights, decision-making and general influence, associated shareholders who vote together, and specific conditions in a shareholders' agreement can result in control being exercised by a minority shareholder. Something to watch out for when investing or contracting with start-ups.

Cottage Business or Industry (aka niche business or industry)

A business that is not massively scalable. These can be very lucrative for the founder as they reach breakeven very quickly but are not always popular with specialist start-up investors as they don't provide the opportunity for high growth multiples.

CPA

Acronym for 'Cost per acquisition'. This model is similar to the 'CPC' but the advertiser only pays when the person viewing the ad actually makes a purchase after clicking on the advert. Costs are generally higher than for CPC but are now directly variable with the sales revenue.

In Australia this is also the acronym for a Certified Practising Accountant; one of the three professional bodies recognised in the accounting field.

CPC

Acronym for 'cost per click'. The way in which much internet advertising is transacted: Adverts are shown on a prospective webpage and the advertiser pays a (usually small) sum to the service provider and/or webpage owner each time a viewer clicks on the advert.

Convertible note

Also known as 'con-note'. This is a way of raising capital without giving away equity at the time. Instead the money is given as a fixed term loan usually with a fixed interest rate agreed between the parties. Interest may be paid or may be added to the value of the note. At the end of the term, or at a pre-agreed performance milestone, the note converts into equity at a pre-agreed rate.

CRM

Customer relationship management. This is a software solution that allows a business to see the history and status of any customer on their database.

Crowd Sourcing

The practice of obtaining funds from a large number of unrelated parties who each invest a small amount. Usually done online: The most well-known platform for this is KickStarter.

Customer development model

Development of products based on the stated needs of the customer followed by the design of a business model to deliver these. The opposite of the 'product development model'. Sometimes called 'customer centric design'.

Deck (aka Pitch Deck)

A brief Powerpoint presentation that covers all aspects of the business in a concise and compelling way. Usually accompanies an information memorandum. Should never replace one!

De-Risking

Closing the accounts of clients that are perceived to be high risk in relation to money laundering or terrorist financing, poor credit or payment practices, or reputational contagion. Should be a regular process for all fast-growing companies.

Dilution

The reduction in percentage of ownership that is suffered by existing shareholders when new equity is issued to other shareholders.

Director

A person who is elected by the shareholders to govern the company on their behalf. The directors form a board and the board oversees the management.

Disruptive Technology (aka game changer)

Something that completely changes the way an industry is structured or the way in which customers often do business. This is a frequently maligned and exaggerated claim and should not be applied to significant improvements in a value chain.

Down Round

A round of capital raising that takes place at a lower price than the round (or rounds) that preceded it. This is not a good thing and usually happens when a business has failed to meet its KPIs or targets.

Due Diligence
(aka DD)

Due diligence is the process of investigating an individual or entity before signing a contract or entering a significant business relationship. Due diligence assesses commercial viability, legal obligations, compliance, risk, and counter-party issues. Due diligence and customer due diligence (CDD) are strictly controlled in FinTechs, and are related to know your customer programs.

Ecosystem (aka Value chain, precinct or cluster)

A convenient noun for the company and its peers, suppliers (including VCs, Angels, etc.), technology partners and grant funders. Usually refers to a specific location (e.g. The Melbourne BioTech Precinct) or industry.

Elevator pitch
(aka 30 second pitch)

A concise and attractive statement of the business benefit or value proposition. Ideally short enough to convey to the target whilst riding in an elevator (lift).

Equity

Technically equity is the value of the assets of a business less the value of the debt. In start-ups 'equity' is often used as a term for 'shares', 'share capital' or the percentage of ownership of the business offered to investors for cash/sweat. Equity usually has associated rights to vote on matters of significance, receive information on the progress and prospects of the company and share proportionally in its profits.

ESG — The environmental, social and governance considerations that investors consider when investing in companies.

ESOP (aka ESP) — Acronym for Employee Share Ownership Plan (or Employee Share Plan).

Executive director — Sometimes referred to as an ED. This is a director who works within the company and has the ability to make decisions that commit the company to courses of action or expenditures. The Managing Director is an executive director and other executive directors normally report to the MD in their day to day roles and to the chairman and whole board in their board role.

Exit Strategy

The strategy the founder will use to leave the business. When raising capital this is generally also a strategy that includes the investors (such as an IPO or trade sale). It is how the business will be cristalised into a cash sum for investors.

FinTech

Acronym for financial technology. Used as a classification for any business involving payments, financing, debt or equity sourcing, accounting and record-keeping, etc.

Flip Up

Establishing a new parent entity, often overseas, to form a holding company above the start-up vehicle. Also sometimes used to describe the process of transitioning a head office or holding company to another jurisdiction.

FMA (First Mover Advantage)

The benefit of being the first business to do what you do in the way your business does it. This should translate to a clear value creator such as a proprietary brand name ('Roller Blades'/'Walkman') or large market share combined with a 'sticky' business model. This can be both a pro and con, as it may be necessary to educate the market, so the sales will cost more than they would in a market with existing established demand.

Founder

Someone who starts a company or business. Co-founders are people who together start a company.

Free Service Period (aka Trial)

The practice of allowing customers to 'try before they buy'; gives prospective customers a brief period of free access to a service after which they are required to commit to a contract for a defined period of time. Often confused with 'Freemium' but actually quite different as there are no customers receiving a free service for a long time.

Freemium

A business model whereby the basic product is provided free and then premium features are offered at price. This marketing strategy is often used in businesses where getting a high market share is essential to success. LinkedIn would be a good example of a Freemium service.

Gamification

Turning a website or product experience into a game that encourages people to use it with rewards of various kinds as they progress.

Generation Z
(aka Gen-Z)

The youngest demographic of people with personal spending power (as opposed to those who rely on parental spending). Loosely defined as those born after 1995.

Grant

Money provided by government or philanthropists for the support of newly started businesses that does not create a right to equity. May take the form of an outright gift, money for a specific purpose, dollar matching of investments, soft loans (repaid slowly or at advantageous rates) or goods in kind.

Greenfields

An opportunity to do business in a space where there are currently no competitors.

Group Think

The collective tendency of group members to adopt each other's norms of behaviour and thought. This can undermine rigorous risk assessment or strategic thinking.

Growth Hacking

The practice of finding quick and easy growth for your business. Gamification, freemium and businesses that rely on viral or social media marketing can all claim to 'growth hack'.

Hack

This term used to be used when data or access had been acquired by surreptitious or illegal use of another businesses' or persons' IT. It is currently used to mean getting something easily and quickly. Sometimes referred to as a 'workaround'.

HNI (aka HNWI)

Acronym for high net worth individual; it refers to a wealthy person usually because they are the target of capital raising.

Hockey Stick

The shape of the growth curve in many start-up companies' financial forecasts. This is the front of the classical 'industry development curve'. Few businesses manage to stay on this track but most start-ups aspire to.

Hustle

Used negatively this word refers to a con, scam or trick. Used positively it refers to taking agency or accountability and getting on with the work; it especially applies to people who are not stopped when faced by a new task.

IM

Acronym for Information Memorandum. A document that provides all the information relevant to an investment. For a private company with few shareholders or for raisings to sophisticated investors it is often possible to use an IM rather than a registered prospectus. In USA this is sometimes referred to as an Offering Memorandum (OM).

IMHO

Acronym for In My Humble Opinion. Rarely humble. Often precedes valid objections to a stated course of action.

Incubator (aka Accelerator)

A centre, holding company or location where start-up company founder receive mentoring, advice, investment and/or other assistance

"My approach tends to be revolutionary."

Independent director

An independent director is one who has not major tie to the company other than their director role. This is often specifically defined in each jurisdiction. In Australia an independent director is one who has no material contractual relationship including as a customer, supplier, employee, shareholder or related party to a customer, supplier, shareholder or employee. Many stock exchanges recommend that a majority of directors be independent.

Inflection Point

The point at which cash flows start to flow inwards rather than outwards. Also used to refer to the point at which the business becomes profitable as measured by accounting standards (which can differ substantially from cash flow measures).

Investment round

A distinct process to raise a defined amount of capital (usually within a pre-set time).

IP (aka Intellectual Property)

This can be a patent, design, copyright, or a secret sauce or formula ('Coca Cola' or '11 herbs and spices'). Every start-up has IP. For some this is a crucial part of the business model and must be protected. For others it is simple know how and resides in the way the business is structured or the relationships it has with other industry participants.

Iterate (aka Trial and Error)

A strategy where the business will try something, do it wrong, and try it again in a slightly different way in the hope of a better result.

Know Your Customer (aka KYC)

In Banks and FinTechs: Anti-money laundering policies and procedures used to determine the true identity of a customer and the type of activity that is normal and expected. KYC software should detect activity that is 'unusual' for a particular customer.

In brokering and Investment Advice: the requirement for an advisor to know the risk appetite of the principal and only recommend appropriate investments, policies and courses of action.

KPI

Key Performance Indicator – a measure of success in a strategically relevant indicator. User numbers, revenue, profit or share price are common KPIs.

Launch

To start a company, introduce a product to a market or put a website online.

Lead Investor

The one in each round that is investing the greatest amount. This investor may often set the terms upon which all the others invest. This can include setting aside equity for employee compensation, limiting the decision-making capacity of the board and/or founders, allocating themselves or others a board seat, and even setting special clauses giving pre-emptive rights in takeovers or other activities.

Lean Startup

A lean start-up proves the business concept as quickly and cheaply as possible. These businesses frequently use outsourced suppliers for much of the work and, whilst the concept is proven, can prove hard to control as competitors can replicate due to the lack of proprietary IP. The concept of 'lean' is derived from Toyota's 'lean manufacturing' which aimed to maximise productivity whilst minimising waste.

Leverage

When used as a verb (to leverage/will leverage) it is the process of using something — technology, partnerships, market relationships — to full (and surprisingly high) advantage. When used as a noun (has leverage/applies leverage) it is the possession of a market position or technology platform that enables quick and easy success.

LOL

Acronym for Lots of Laughs, this is not a compliment.

Loss Leader Pricing

To sell one product or service at a loss as a form of marketing expense to entice customers to enter into a relationship that can then be 'leveraged' to sell them other products and services at a profit. Sometimes takes the form of an initial 'free service period' prior to a commitment.

Low Hanging Fruit

Something that is easy and profitable that a company can do to generate cash before moving on to more difficult tasks. Highly desirable if pursuing a 'boot strapping' strategy. Often hard to identify.

Managing Director

A board member upon whom the other board members have delegated the task of running the company. Unlike the CEO the Managing Director (or MD) has a vote in board decisions.

Market Penetration

The percentage of the total potential market the company aims to capture within a given timeframe. Important to justify both the size of the market and the probability of achieving such penetration with independent data.

"Did anyone else bring his thinking cap."

Market Segment (aka segment)

A clearly defined group of potential customers for a given product. As a general rule a business should know what market it is in (e.g. the online education space) and segment that market (e.g. by geographic location, by socio-economic classification, by level of prior learning, by length of course, etc.) before targeting a segment that is highly prospective (e.g. tertiary qualified professionals) with a product or service (e.g. an online course with an accredited qualification upon completion) that provides a perceived benefit (e.g. general business skills).

Monetize

The strategy for turning activity into cash; how the business plans to make money. Very important to articulate clearly for premium or loss leader strategies.

Money Laundering

The process of concealing or disguising the existence, source, movement, destination or illegal application of illicitly-derived property or funds to make them appear legitimate. It may involve a three-part system: placement of funds into a financial system; layering of transactions to disguise the source, ownership and location of the funds; and integration of the funds into society in the form of holdings that appear legitimate

MVP (Minimum Viable Product)

In manufacturing this is the smallest production run that will allow a profit to be made. It is a function of the relative proportions of fixed and variable costs. Where costs are 100% variable the MVP = 1. In modern technology businesses this term is used instead of 'prototype' to refer to the first version of a product required to achieve proof of concept. Often used in the creation of new software that will be Beta tested, and later upgraded with extra features.

NDA/CA Acronym for Non-Disclosure Agreement or Confidentiality agreement. A binding contract between two parties whereby the person receiving information (usually to enable assessment of the investment potential) is required to maintain the confidentiality of the information. Breaches can involve significant damages and legal action.

Non-executive director (aka NED or outside director) A director who has no executive role in the company. A NED can only make decisions for the company in the context of a resolution of the whole board. There is no requirement for a shareholder to be a NED or for a NED to own shares.

NPV

Acronym for net present value which is the value of future cash-flows discounted by a factor to give an approximation of what they are worth at the current date. The factor is known as a discount rate and is highly contested in negotiations.

Offshoring

Moving a company's registered address overseas to benefit from trading efficiencies, lower tax rates (tax havens) or laxer corporate laws. Common tax havens include Bermuda, British Virgin Islands and the Cayman Islands. Singapore and Hong Kong are sometimes favoured for their logistics. States (such as Delaware in the USA) can be considered "offshore", even if this is not literally true geographically.

OPM

Acronym for Other people's Money; high on OPM is a phrase for cash rich businesses that are acquiring others in a 'roll up' or amalgamation strategy.

Option

The right to acquire a share at a future date usually at a specified price but sometimes at a price calculated according to a specified formula (such as a multiple of profit). Options are often used to incentivise management to perform.

Percentage of market

The usually unfounded dream of start-ups addressing mass markets (typified by statements such as "if we capture 1% of the market the company will be huge…"). It is crucial to back this argument with segmentation and targeting that gives credence to the likelihood of success. It is generally more credible to access a large percentage of a small defined market than a small percentage of a large amorphous one.

"What if we don't change at all … and something magical just happens?"

Pivot

To completely change direction. Often occurs after a disastrous trial and error process or failed iteration but is also sometimes used when a company that is successful discovers a way to be even more successful. This term can be used by an established company seeking to serve a different market segment or using its established technology/skills in a different way.

Placement

Issue of shares to one, or a few, large investors without an offer to all shareholders or the general public.

Politically Exposed People (aka PEPs)

An individual deemed to be potentially corruptible because of their position of influence in government or public sphere, or strong links to people in government. It is not illegal to do business with PEPs, or to be one. Companies and their boards should at least be aware if a PEP owns, part-owns or is a director their company or a business partner.

Pre-money valuation

Also known as 'the pre-money' or 'the pre'. The amount a company is worth before it raises capital.

President

A director who chairs the board and manages the company. This is a big concentration of power in the hands of one individual and many professional investors reject this arrangement.

Product development model

Development of products and design of a business model to identify potential customers and offer the product to them. The opposite of the 'customer development model'.

Prospectus

A registered document that enables the issuing company to solicit investment from retail investors. This is a complex legal document and must be factually correct as well as complete in the information it provides. Because retail investors are deemed 'unsophisticated' it must be written clearly and spell out risks as well as expected returns.

Prototype

A working example of a product that allows potential investors and/or customers to see how it works and looks.

Quorum

The minimum number of people required to pass a resolution or constitute a valid meeting. It will be stated in the constitution.

Ramen Profitable

Refers to the stage where a company is profitable enough to cover costs and basic living expenses for everyone working at a startup. The term comes from the urban myth that entrepreneurs can live cheaply on ramen noodles whilst waiting for their companies to succeed. No dietician has verified that myth.

Responsive Design

Originally used to describe services that are tailored to the user as the users' needs become apparent. Commonly applied to the design of websites that look good when viewed on multiple devices (phones, tablets, desktops). It works by resizing text and images to suit the dimensions of the screen upon which it is viewed.

Retail Investor

(aka Mums and Dads)

Not a sophisticated investor: in many jurisdictions there are stringent rules about marketing to retail investor and these will require disclosures akin to those included in a prospectus for an exchange listing.

Rights Issue

Issue of shares to the existing shareholders with each having the right to buy new equity at a quantum that is proportional to their current stake. Rights issues are 'non-dilutionary' as each shareholder retains their existing proportion of ownership if they choose to participate.

Companies may choose if they wish to allow unused rights (forfeited by shareholders who do not take up the offer) to other existing or new shareholders.

ROI

Acronym for Return On Investment. What the investor can expect to get for what they put in. Often cited in multiples of the original sum invested (a ten times ROI) or as a percentage that is gained each year (30% ROI is approximately a ten time ROI given a ten year investment horizon).
It can also be used to describe success of a marketing campaign's and, if so, it is important to specify the time frame and whether the measure is sales or profits.
A negative ROI is a loss.

RSS (RDF site summary, or Rich Site Summary, or Really Simple Sindication)

A way to easily distribute a list of headlines, update notices, and sometimes content to a wide number of people. It is used by computer programs that organize those headlines and notices for easy reading.

Also a type of web feed which allows users and applications to access updates to online content in a standardized, computer-readable format.

Runway

Describes the amount of time a business has at the current 'burn rate' until the cash runs out and either new capital must be raised or operations must cease.

SaaS

Acronym for Software As A Service. A business does not sell software but licenses or leases it through a subscription model.

Scaleable

Something that can grow quickly to a massive market because the demand is big enough or because it can move into different markets via 'Pivoting' or 'Iterating'.

Secretariat

The group of people supporting a board. In a small company this is usually comprised of very few individuals. Typical secretariat members include the Company Secretary, CEO, CFO, General or Legal Counsel, and the CEO's or Chairman's executive assistant.

Search Engine Optimization
(aka SEO)

The process of analyzing website and social media content to enhance its discoverability and ranking in search engines such as Google. Ranking is based upon sophisticated algorithms which change frequently and are not published by the engine owners. Consultants use trial and error to discover changes that increase discoverability and this can be an expensive iterative process.

Seed Round

The very first round of external funding which is typically performed at a low valuation to raise funds which will assist in reaching the point of readiness for the next capital raise (which is the Series A Round).

Series A Round Shareholders' Agreement

Usually the second (but occasionally the first) round of external capital raising.

A contract that sets out the rights and duties of the company and its early shareholders. Typically this includes voting powers, dilution events, matters reserved for the shareholders, appointment of directors to the board, etc.

"First, the Rules of Engagement for this meeting ..."

Sophisticated Investor (aka Accredited investor – particularly in USA)

The definition changes depending on where you live but here in Australia you'll fall under the Corporations Act 2001. To be considered a sophisticated or wholesale investor you need to meet at least one of the following benchmarks:

- Have proof of net assets of more than $2.5m;
- Have proof of income of at least $250k over the last two financial years;
- Are investing $500k or more into the opportunity.

Proof should be provided by a certified accountant. In general, if you don't meet at least one of the above, you will be deemed to be a retail investor.

Space

Originally used to define a specific physical location (e.g. office space, floor space, meeting space) and now used to define industry segments (e.g. the online betting space, the healthy fast food space). Particularly used by businesses that exist as online purchase and/or delivery mechanisms. Also referred to as a field, vertical or segment.

Special General Meeting

Sometimes referred to as an extraordinary general meeting or by the acronyms EGM/SGM. This is a meeting convened for a special or extraordinary purpose rather than as a standard annual reporting forum.

Strategic plan

A highly aspirational plan that describes and costs the activities and details the desired outcomes over a long term time frame.

Sweat Equity

Shares in the company (or a specific subsidiary) company given in exchange for work done. This is often used to attract talented staff and preserve cash by reducing the amount of salary paid to balance the value of the equity. When combined with vesting, escrow and cliff periods it is also a good way to retain key staff by disincentivising them from leaving.

Target market
(aka target)

The particular 'market segment' that a business aims to serve with its products and/or services.

Term Sheet (aka investment overview and shareholder agreement)

The document that outlines what the Investors will get for what they put in — including % ownership, board representation and voting rights.

Traction — Track record in a real market; proof that customers will actually buy the product or service.

Trigger — An event or action that causes another event or action. Most commonly used in relation to vesting or equity incentives or options.

UI (aka UX) — Acronym for User Interface (or User eXperience). Particularly common in software and internet commerce ventures.

Up Round — A round of fund raising that takes place at a higher share price than its predecessors. This is the desired normal practice and usually indicates that a business has been meeting its KPIs.

Valuation

What a company is thought to be worth. "Pre-money valuation" is the value before investors' cash is received. "Post-money valuation" is the pre-money valuation amount plus the investment amount.

Value Proposition

The benefits attained by customers that make a business, service or product uniquely attractive. It is possible to have more than one value proposition or to have different value propositions for each customer. Note that this is different to 'feature' or 'function'; it is the value to the user rather than an inherent attribute of the product or service itself.

Vaporware

A product that does not yet exist (and may never exist). It is a way to test market demand. Vaporware will sell at a discount to products that have 'traction'.

VC

Acronym for Venture Capital or Venture Capitalist. A person, business or investment vehicle that makes investments in other companies. VCs specialise in the types of company that they fund. Many VCs have rules about board representation, burn rate, runway, sweat equity, escrow periods, and exit strategies. VCs normally enter as investors after the business model is proven through an MVP, prototype, or operating successfully on a smaller scale (as is the case for many franchised businesses).

Vesting period The period of time before a person who has been granted shares (either as 'sweat equity' or through a performance, loyalty or assisted share purchase scheme) actually receives title to the shares. It is common for performance shares to vest in tranches to increase the loyalty incentive associated with their ownership and help retain high-performing staff.

Viral (aka viral advertising) A product or service that becomes known to prospective customers because others (usually unpaid although sometimes the process starts with paid 'celebrity' placements or endorsements). It is a new term for rapidly-spread word-of-mouth.

Workaround

A solution developed for a problem that has arisen during the implementation stage of a strategy. Sometimes also used for a process that makes something easier, cheaper or faster.

About the Author

This glossary of start-up terminology definitions was prepared by Julie Garland McLellan.

It is a good humoured guide to, and not a definitive legal ruling on, the current commonly understood meaning of the terms included. If you have an alternative meaning for any of the terms or wish to volunteer an additional term for inclusion please contact Julie via email at julie@mclellan.com.au

Julie Garland-McLellan is a company director and chairman with experience on a range of not-for-profit, public sector and commercial boards, both listed and private. She has experienced start-ups, turnarounds and everything in between!

Julie is an international expert on board governance. Her newsletter The Director's Dilemma™ is read in 36 different countries. Subscribe at
http://www.directorsdilemma.com

Julie is a former council member for the Australian Institute of Company Directors; and, as well as facilitating, she has developed many of their courses. Julie has a degree in Civil Engineering, an executive MBA, a certificate in Entrepreneurship, and a diploma and advanced diploma in Company Directorship.

Julie is the author of 5 books on governance:

- Presenting to Boards;
- Dilemmas, Dilemmas: Practical case studies for company directors;
- Dilemmas, Dilemmas II: More practical case studies for company directors;
- Not-for-Profit Board Dilemmas; and
- All Above Board: Great Governance for the Government Sector.

Cartoons in this book are supplied courtesy of Shutterstock.com

START UP TERMINOLOGY

www.ingramcontent.com/pod-product-compliance
Lightning Source LLC
Chambersburg PA
CBHW040235220526
45473CB00001B/257